#MeToo

Unveiling Abuse

Megan Borgert-Spaniol

Abdo & Daughters

An Imprint of Abdo Publishing
abdobooks.com

abdobooks.com

Published by Abdo Publishing, a division of ABDO, PO Box 398166, Minneapolis, Minnesota 55439. Copyright © 2020 by Abdo Consulting Group, Inc. International copyrights reserved in all countries. No part of this book may be reproduced in any form without written permission from the publisher. Abdo & Daughters™ is a trademark and logo of Abdo Publishing.

Printed in the United States of America, North Mankato, Minnesota
052019
092019

Design: Aruna Rangarajan, Mighty Media, Inc.
Production: Mighty Media, Inc.
Editor: Liz Salzmann
Cover Photographs: Shutterstock
Interior Photographs: Design elements, Shutterstock; Alamy, p. 7; AP Images, pp. 14–15, 19; Getty Images, pp. 8, 26; Shutterstock, pp. 3, 5, 10 (inset), 10–11, 12–13, 16–17, 20–21, 23, 24–25, 28 (top), 28 (bottom left), 28 (bottom right), 29 (top), 29 (bottom)

Library of Congress Control Number: 2018966453

Publisher's Cataloging-in-Publication Data
Names: Borgert-Spaniol, Megan, author.
Title: #MeToo: unveiling abuse / by Megan Borgert-Spaniol
Other title: Unveiling abuse
Description: Minneapolis, Minnesota : Abdo Publishing, 2020 | Series: #Movements | Includes online resources and index.
Identifiers: ISBN 9781532119316 (lib. bdg.) | ISBN 9781532173776 (ebook)
Subjects: LCSH: Sexual harassment--United States--Juvenile literature. | Reporting of rape--Juvenile literature. | Sexual abuse victims--Legal status, laws, etc--Juvenile literature. | Protest movements--Juvenile literature.
Classification: DDC 323--dc23

CONTENTS

It was a Sunday in October 2017. Actress Alyssa Milano was relaxing at home. It had been a difficult week for her and other members of the entertainment industry. Several Hollywood actresses had accused a well-known movie producer of sexual harassment and sexual assault.

Posts about the accusations filled social media. Milano was inspired by a Facebook post. The post suggested that anyone who had been sexually harassed or assaulted post "Me too" on Facebook. This would show how widespread the problem was. Milano wanted to spread this message. So, she posted about it on Twitter. She invited those who had experienced sexual harassment or assault to reply, "Me too."

LET'S TALK TERMS

Sexual harassment is any unwelcome spoken or physical behavior of a sexual nature. Sexual assault is any sexual contact that occurs without consent. Giving consent means actively and clearly agreeing to participate in sexual activity.

By the next morning, tens of thousands of people had replied to Milano's tweet. Most of the posts were from women. Some shared their stories. Others simply replied, "Me too." The phrase became a hashtag. #MeToo was all over social media, including Facebook, Twitter, and Instagram. It was the beginning of a movement that quickly spread across the nation and the world.

In October 2018, Milano attended *Variety* magazine's Power of Women lunch in California. The event honored women who have made a difference in various causes and charities.

The hashtag #MeToo exploded overnight. But sexual harassment and assault were not new. They have existed for centuries. Historically, in most societies, men have held a higher status than women. This was true at home, in the workplace, and in government. As a result, men have had greater access to positions of power.

One mark of this unequal status was separate gender roles. In the past, women were considered unfit to hold paying jobs. So, they took care of their homes while their fathers and husbands earned money. However, many single women needed jobs to survive. These women often worked in factories or as maids or servants. Many women experienced sexual harassment and assault from the men they worked with. But because the women had a lower status, they had little power to fight their abusers.

Over time, gender roles shifted. More women were fighting for higher social status. One key to gaining higher status is the ability to support oneself financially. Through the 1900s, the number of women joining the workforce steadily climbed.

Even as women fought for higher social status, men still held more power. And many women continued to face sexual harassment and assault. But before the 1970s, Americans didn't openly discuss these issues. The term *sexual harassment* didn't even exist yet.

Rosie the Riveter became a symbol of working women during World War II. Many women took over jobs left by men who went to fight in the war.

Groups including the Women's Legal Defense
Fund and the Working Women's Institute helped
work on Vinson's (*pictured*) case.

In the 1970s, more women were joining the American workforce than ever before. During this time, Lin Farley was teaching a class at Cornell University in Ithaca, New York. The subject of the class was women and work. Many of the students also held jobs. Farley learned that many female students were experiencing physical or emotional pressure or abuse from men they worked with. Farley decided there should be a name for this.

In 1975, Farley spoke at a hearing. It was before the Commission on Human Rights of New York City. At the hearing, Farley talked about women in the workplace. She introduced the term *sexual harassment*. Farley explained how widespread the behavior was in the workplace.

At first, US courts considered sexual harassment a personal matter, not a legal issue. Female activists and lawyers worked to change this. They argued that sexual harassment is a form of sex discrimination, which was already against the law.

Their efforts paved the way for a 1986 US Supreme Court decision in the case of *Meritor Savings Bank v. Vinson*. Mechelle Vinson worked at the bank. She alleged that her supervisor sexually harassed her at work. She said this harassment created a hostile work environment.

The Supreme Court agreed. The justices ruled that "sexual harassment that results in a hostile work environment is a violation of Title VII of the Civil Rights Act of 1964, which bans sex discrimination by employers." This meant employers could now be sued for sexual harassment.

Shamed into Silence

The 1986 Supreme Court ruling was a step in the right direction. But it didn't end the problem. The first sexual harassment case to receive national attention happened in 1991.

That year, judge Clarence Thomas was nominated to the Supreme Court. But before the US Senate approved his nomination, a woman spoke out against him. Her name was Anita Hill. Hill was a law professor who had worked with Thomas years earlier. In a Senate hearing, she accused Thomas of sexually harassing her during their time working together.

Thomas denied Hill's allegations. Enough senators believed Thomas over Hill that Thomas was voted onto the Supreme Court. Meanwhile, Hill was publicly shamed and criticized for her accusations. She even received death threats.

Clarence Thomas

Hill's testimony brought the issue of sexual harassment into the national spotlight. But it also showed what often happens when a victim comes forward. The backlash to Hill's testimony sent the message that speaking up can be useless and harmful. It reinforced many women's feelings that staying silent is safer.

In 2017, Hill was contacted by the Commission on Sexual Harassment and Advancing Equality in the Workplace. She was asked to lead the commission's work against sexual harassment in the entertainment industry.

Recent polls found that 35 percent of women in the US have been sexually harassed at work.

It is estimated that 75 percent of sexual harassment incidents go unreported. It is also estimated that an even greater percentage of sexual assaults go unreported. Studies have found there are common reasons why people do not report these acts.

Most often, it is fear that keeps victims quiet. Many perpetrators of sexual harassment and assault threaten their victims to silence them. For example, victims have been told they will lose their jobs if they report their experiences. Perpetrators have also threatened victims with violence.

The silence surrounding sexual harassment has made the behavior hard to identify. Some victims say they weren't sure whether their experiences were sexual harassment or assault. In fact, many of these victims say they considered the behavior normal or "the way things are." Such cases are evidence of the acceptance of sexual harassment throughout society.

Fear, uncertainty, and acceptance have long kept victims of sexual harassment and assault silent. But in 2017, that silence began to break in a way it never had before.

TAGGED

"I am grateful today, to be alive, for all those I love, and for all those who have the courage to stand up for others…#metoo"
—actress Uma Thurman
(@umathurman, Instagram)

Unveiling Abuse

Starting in 2017, sexual harassment and assault were commonly talked about. In January, Donald Trump became president of the United States. Before his election, the *Washington Post* released a 2005 video of Trump talking about sexually assaulting women. He said he could get away with it because he was famous.

Trump was publicly condemned for his comments. But he still received enough votes to win the 2016 presidential election. This sparked anger across the nation. Many Americans were shocked that a person who spoke casually about sexual assault could be elected president.

The national conversation about sexual harassment continued as other powerful people were accused of it. Sexual harassment and assault were being exposed at some large companies. These companies included Uber and FOX News.

In fall 2017, attention turned to Hollywood. On October 5, the *New York Times* published an article about movie producer Harvey Weinstein. In the article, several women accused Weinstein of sexual harassment and assault. They said this behavior took place over nearly thirty years. Days later, similar accusations from more women were published in an article in the *New Yorker*. Many of Weinstein's accusers were well-known Hollywood actresses. And for many, the experiences they reported had occurred

Actress Rose McGowan was one of the women mentioned in the *New York Times* article about Weinstein. She also talks about her experiences with Weinstein in her memoir, *Brave*.

ROSE McGOWA

The revelations about Weinstein (*left*) led to his arrest for sexual assault.

when they were starting their careers. Their stories showed how Weinstein had abused his power as a movie producer.

As more women shared their experiences, other survivors started to speak out. Each person knew they weren't just one voice accusing a powerful person. Instead, they were one of many voices. This made it easier to come forward. Because these women were public figures, it was easy for them to reach a large audience. But most victims do not have that opportunity.

This changed on October 15 when Milano created her Twitter post. Milano had experienced sexual harassment and assault herself. She wanted to help bring victims together in solidarity. Her post said, "If you've been sexually harassed or assaulted, write 'me too' as a reply to this tweet." By the next day, "Me Too" had become a hashtag. It had been tweeted nearly half a million times. It had also been shared on Facebook in more than 12 million posts, comments, and reactions.

#MeToo had taken over social media. It showed how common sexual harassment and assault is. A movement of unveiling abuse had begun.

The Silence Breakers

In one week, the #MeToo hashtag spread to 85 countries around the world. While Milano's tweet sparked this social media movement, a similar "Me Too" movement already existed. It was started in 2006 by activist Tarana Burke. Burke had used the phrase "Me Too" in a community campaign. This campaign supported women and girls who had survived sexual violence.

Milano learned about the earlier "Me Too" campaign shortly after her tweet went viral. She contacted Burke to join forces. And in a TV interview, Milano credited Burke's years of work in the movement. Burke and Milano both played a part in starting a movement. But Burke later pointed out that "Me Too" is bigger than her and Milano. "Neither of us should be centered in this work," she said. "This is about survivors."

During the months after #MeToo started, victims of sexual harassment and assault continued to speak out. While the majority of victims were women, men were coming forward too. Among them was actor Terry Crews. He shared his experience of sexual assault on Twitter. As a result of victims speaking out, their perpetrators were facing consequences. Weinstein was just one of many perpetrators whose careers came to an end. Guilty public figures were quitting or getting fired from their positions. Some faced criminal charges.

THE FACE OF #METOO

Tarana Burke

Tarana Burke is an activist and community organizer from New York City. She is also a survivor of sexual violence. For Burke, the phrase "Me Too" was a way of connecting to other survivors. So, in 2006, she created a "Me Too" campaign to let victims know they are not alone.

After #MeToo went viral in 2017, many Twitter users called attention to Burke's earlier work in the movement. Burke joined the conversation, expressing support for all the people saying "Me Too." She also noted that the movement went far beyond social media.

"It's beyond a hashtag. It's the start of a larger conversation and a movement for radical community healing. Join us. #metoo"
—Tarana Burke
(@TaranaBurke, Twitter)

Singer-songwriter Taylor Swift was one of six women pictured on the cover of *Time* magazine's Silence Breakers issue.

In December 2017, *Time* magazine named "The Silence Breakers" as the 2017 Person of the Year. The magazine was referring to all the people who spoke out in the #MeToo movement. The *Time* article featured some celebrities who had shared their experiences of sexual harassment and assault. But it also featured farmworkers, housekeepers, and professors who had been victims. It showed that sexual harassment and abuse exists across all industries.

TAGGED

"One tweet has brought together 1.7 million voices from 85 countries. Standing side by side, together, our movement will only grow. #MeToo"
—Alyssa Milano
(@Alyssa_Milano, Twitter)

#TimesUp

After a year of unveiling abuse, 2018 began with a sense of hope and determination. On January 1, more than 300 Hollywood women formed an initiative. They called it Time's Up. Its purpose is to fight sexual harassment in Hollywood and beyond.

The spirit of Time's Up and #MeToo was present at award ceremonies in early 2018. At January's Golden Globe Awards, many stars wore black clothing. This was to show solidarity with victims of sexual harassment and assault. Two months later, actresses Ashley Judd, Annabella Sciorra, and Salma Hayek took the stage at the Academy Awards. They spoke about the power of voices joining together.

Beyond Hollywood, voices continued to join together. A second annual Women's March took place on January 20, 2018. The first had occurred the day after Trump's inauguration in 2017. In 2018, more than one million protestors from around the country marched. Many of them held signs with the hashtags #MeToo and #TimesUp. These movements were the reason many of the participants decided to march.

TAGGED

"Dressed in all black . Proud . Loud . In solidarity. #WHYWEWEARBLACK #TIMESUP"
—singer and actress Janelle Monáe (@JanelleMonae, Twitter)

San Francisco, California, was one of hundreds of cities in the US and around the world that held protests on January 20, 2018.

Continuing Conversation

The #MeToo movement changed the way many Americans viewed sexual harassment and assault. As Milano had hoped, #MeToo showed how widespread the problem is. #MeToo was an important step for victims too. It did what Burke set out to do with her 2006 "Me Too" campaign.

#MeToo showed victims that they aren't alone. It showed they can rely on the support of their communities. This support helped victims share the shame they felt. And as Burke pointed out, it "put the shame where it belongs: on the perpetrator."

As with any movement, #MeToo has had critics. One criticism is that when accusations are made on social media, they spread quickly. Because of this, critics argue, accused individuals are publicly condemned before they can defend themselves. Critics feel this is unfair.

It is especially troublesome when the behavior is hard to define. What some people consider sexual harassment or abuse, others may simply view as just immature or thoughtless behavior. But supporters of the movement note that targeting this behavior is necessary. It helps continue the conversation about what consent means

Shortly after the #MeToo movement started, actor Kevin Spacey was accused of making unwanted sexual advances toward several men. This led to him being fired from the TV show *House of Cards*.

and how to tell whether someone has given consent. In spite of criticisms, #MeToo has helped bring justice to both victims and perpetrators.

In April 2018, the *New York Times* and the *New Yorker* were recognized for helping the #MeToo movement. The publications were awarded the Pulitzer Prize for reporting the stories of Weinstein's accusers in 2017. This reporting was considered a public service. It set off a worldwide conversation that sparked hope and inspiration.

"But hope and inspiration are only sustained by work," Burke says. This includes the work of healing for victims of sexual harassment and assault. It is also the work of communities trying to support victims. And, it is the work of changing society's attitudes about both women and men.

The work of #MeToo will take time. As Anita Hill has pointed out, "…we're kidding ourselves if we think that everything is going to change overnight…." Hill didn't have the support of #MeToo when she shared her experiences in 1991. But the conversation she started back then continues. The work of #MeToo will persist long after the hashtag fades.

One of *Time* magazine's Silence Breakers was Susan Fowler. She had been harassed while working at rideshare company Uber. In the article, she says, "There's something really empowering about standing up for what's right."

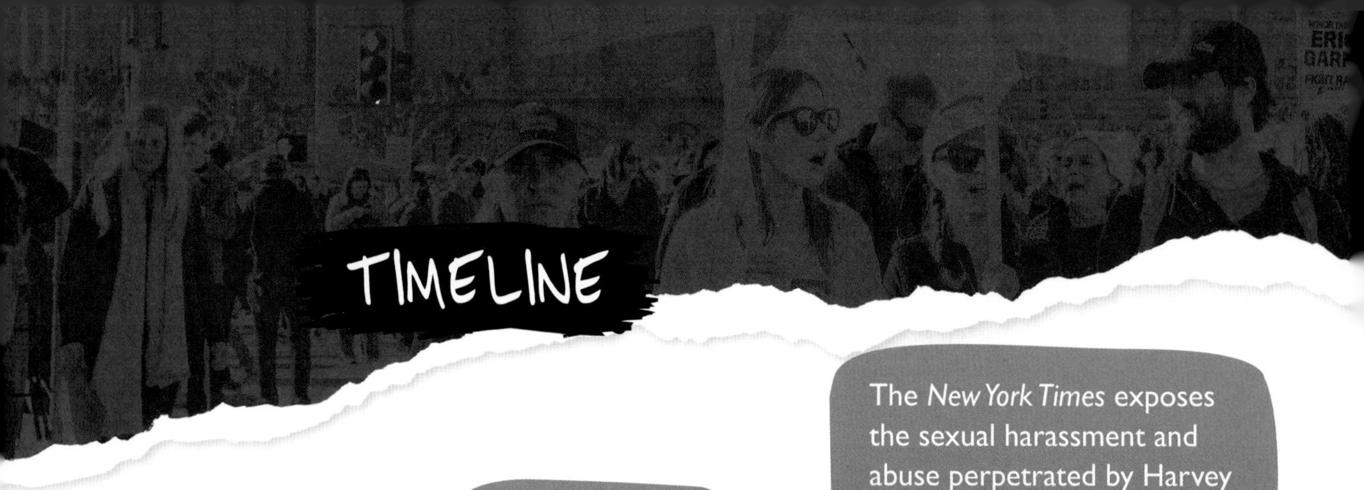

TIMELINE

Lin Farley introduces the term *sexual harassment.*

1975

Anita Hill accuses Supreme Court nominee Clarence Thomas of sexual harassment.

1991

The *New York Times* exposes the sexual harassment and abuse perpetrated by Harvey Weinstein. Many of the women accusing Weinstein are Hollywood actresses.

October 5, 2017

1986

A US Supreme Court ruling declares sexual harassment in the workplace illegal.

2006

Activist Tarana Burke starts a campaign to support survivors of sexual violence using the phrase "Me Too."

Actress Alyssa Milano suggests on Twitter that victims of sexual harassment and assault post the words "Me too." A #MeToo hashtag goes viral within 24 hours.

More than 300 women form Time's Up, an initiative to fight sexual harassment in Hollywood and beyond.

The *New York Times* and the *New Yorker* are awarded the Pulitzer Prize for their 2017 reporting about Harvey Weinstein.

October 15, 2017

January 1, 2018

April 2018

December 2017

January 20, 2018

Time magazine names "The Silence Breakers" the 2017 Person of the Year.

Protesters attend the second annual Women's March to show support for #MeToo and #TimesUp.

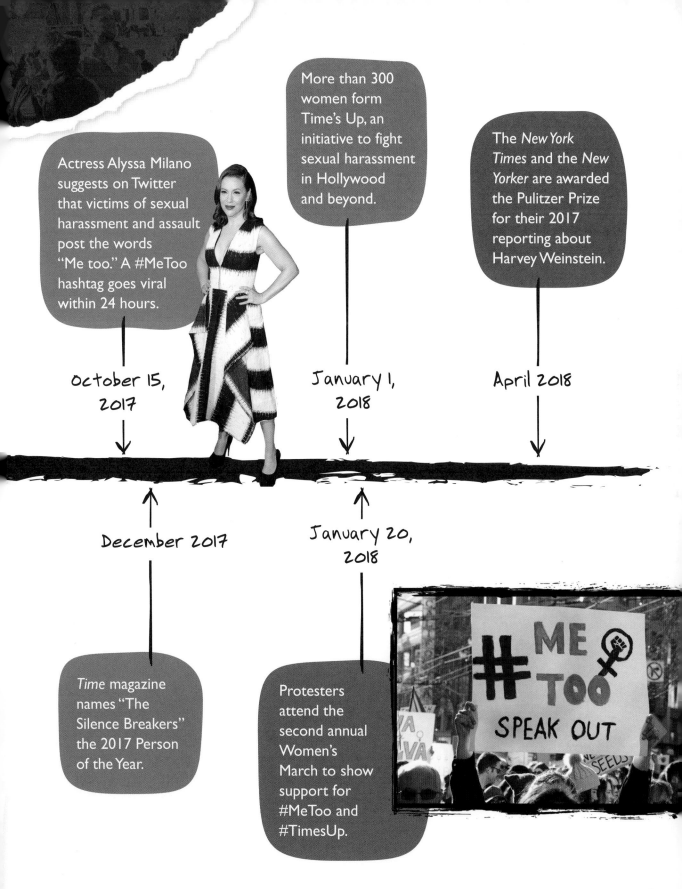

ME TOO SPEAK OUT

GLOSSARY

Academy Awards—an event where the Academy of Motion Picture Arts and Sciences gives awards to the best actors and filmmakers of the year.

activist—a person who takes direct action in support of or in opposition to an issue that causes disagreement.

audience—a group of readers, listeners, or spectators.

backlash—a strong public reaction against something.

define—to describe or explain something.

discrimination—unfair treatment, often based on race, religion, or gender.

gender roles—the idea that certain activities, jobs, and behaviors are only for women or only for men.

Golden Globe Award—an award recognizing excellence in both the movie and television industries.

harass—to annoy or bother someone again and again. This behavior is called harassment.

hashtag—a word or phrase used in social media posts, such as tweets, that starts with the symbol # and that briefly indicates what the post is about.

inauguration—a ceremony in which a person is sworn into a political office.

initiative—a plan or program that is intended to solve a problem.

participate—to take part or share in something. Someone who participates is a participant.

perpetrate—to do something, usually something that is wrong or illegal. Someone who perpetrates something is a perpetrator.

Pulitzer Prize—one of several annual awards established by journalist Joseph Pulitzer. The awards honor accomplishments in journalism, literature, drama, and music.

social media—websites or smartphone apps that provide information and entertainment and allow people to communicate with each other. Facebook and Twitter are examples of social media.

solidarity—a feeling of unity between people who have the same interests, goals, or experiences.

status—a social or professional standing, position, or rank.

Supreme Court—the highest, most powerful court in the United States.

viral—quickly or widely spread, usually by electronic communication.

ONLINE RESOURCES

Booklinks
NONFICTION NETWORK
FREE! ONLINE NONFICTION RESOURCES

To learn more about #MeToo, please visit **abdobooklinks.com** or scan this QR code. These links are routinely monitored and updated to provide the most current information available.

INDEX